It's Still A Wonderful World

COLORFUL MUSINGS FROM THE MIND OF HARLEY WHITE SR.

Archway Publishing books may be ordered through booksellers or by contacting:

Archway Publishing
1663 Liberty Drive
Bloomington, IN 47403
www.archwaypublishing.com
844-669-3957

ISBN: 978-1-6657-4669-4 (sc)
ISBN: 978-1-6657-4671-7 (hc)
ISBN: 978-1-6657-4670-0 (e)

Library of Congress Control Number: 2023912931

Print information available on the last page.

Archway Publishing rev. date: 03/27/2023

Foreword

This book is a collection of thoughts and statements about life and its revelations to me personally. As a professional jazz bassist musician for over sixty years who traveled around the world, playing with well-known jazz and gospel artists, I often found myself in unusual circumstances at times. For example, in 1975 when playing with Earl "Fatha" Hines at a tribute to Earl "Fatha" Hines, sponsored by the Hot Club of France in Orange, France, there we were in a coliseum cave built by Augustus Caesar in the second century, one year after Christ died. This cave was where the lions were kept, and there was little ventilation. While the 200-member audience smoked herb leaf clove cigarettes that had a powerful smell, and swooned to the sounds of the piano, saxophone, drums, vocalist and my bass, the band was gifted 20 loaves of fine and rare cheeses, and all six brands of Johnny Walker Red. After performing, several of us in the band got drunk for the first time, and still received a standing ovation from the audience.

I played in jazz bands while serving in the United States Air Force in the early 1960's in Japan. As a music educator, I had the privilege of teaching middle school students to play musical instruments and perform as an award-winning marching band. These kids were amazing and eager to learn. Later in my career, I was a high school Music Director, I taught high school choir, piano classes, jazz big band, concert band and symphony orchestra.

I relish all these experiences, teaching in schools and colleges, worldwide travel, performing with well-known gospel and jazz artists, performing with local jazz artists, symphonies, and concert bands, holding public office on a college board at one point. Everything has added up to becoming a part of who I am. My provocative observations about life, has come to me in the form of questions and statements. I started a diary and recorded my thoughts. All the visuals were inspired by and for the amusement of the author, and make the musings come to life for the readers to enjoy and think about. This book is intended for those who can appreciate the lighter side of life and to provoke thought about domestic and social issues. This book is dedicated to my family.

Harley

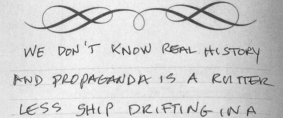

WE DON'T KNOW REAL HISTORY
AND PROPAGANDA IS A RUTTER
LESS SHIP DRIFTING IN A
CLOUD OF ~~FEAR~~

WHAT IS THERE TO LIKE ABOUT
PEOPLE WHO FORCE HARDSHIPS
ON YOUNG FAMILIES THAT THEY
CANNOT BEAR FROM BEHIND
FANCY DESKS IN BANKS?

WALLS ARE BUILT TO
FALL AND FAIL WITH TIME.

THE BASS

IT IS SAID THAT IT CAN BRING
ABOUT DEAFENING APPLAUSE
OR INSPIRE A WILD DANCING
PARTY. SOMETIMES IT CAN
HELP MAKE TEARS, TOO.
SOME PEOPLE CARRY IT
AROUND ALL THEIR LIVES
AND SUFFER CHRONIC
BACK ACHES.

HOW MANY WRONGS DOES IT
TAKE TO MAKE A RIGHT?

DIVERSITY IS NORMALITY.

Photo of a page from Harley's handwritten journal

We don't know real history and propaganda is a rudderless ship drifting in a cloud of fear.

"History"

dreams

What is there to like about people who force hardships on young families that they cannot bear, from behind fancy desks in banks?

"Hardship"

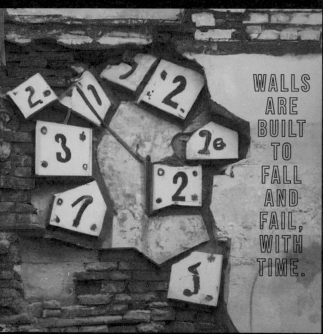

WALLS ARE BUILT TO FALL AND FAIL, WITH TIME.

"Walls"

GHT RIGHT

HOW MANY WRONGS DOES IT TAKE TO MAKE A RIGHT?

"Right"

Bassists

True love,
demands
acceptance of
evolution and
change, openly

"True Love"

Imagine
existing
while
black

"Black"

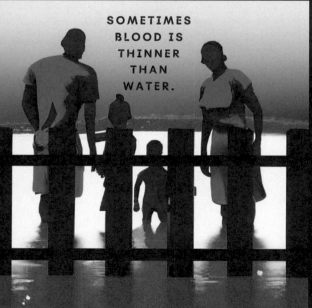

"Blood"

"Books"

"Brutality"

CHERISH DIVERSITY OR
PERISH FROM BOREDOM.

"Cherish"

Church is within you,
and outside you.
Be careful
where
you sit.

"Church"

Bring back high
school civics, or
perish as a
democracy.

"Civics"

A peaceful existence must be earned through experience.

Existence

Imagine, "growing folks" music

Growing

Innovation only occurs with the tolerance of free speech.

Innovation

Undivided attention is profitable.

Attention

The climate is unconcerned about man's economic prosperity and mythology. The wages of sin is death by pollution.

"Climate"

"Colored people is a state of mind and is mythology based."

"Colored People"

Music is concrete magic.

"Concrete"

Condemn no one.

For they could become what you said, and burden you with their fate.

"Condemn"

VOTE FOR THE ONE THAT REJECTS CORPORATIONS AS LIVING PEOPLE WITH MONEY THAT NEVER DIES.

NOVEMBER 9, 2016

"Corporations"

Imagine, having to start your culture over from nothing but vague memories, and relying on creativity to define your future.

"Culture"

There is a thick ring of debris circling the earth that is a disgusting legacy and display of the progression of humanity's ignorance....And it's ingenuity.

"Debris"

DEBT IS SOCIALIZED, AND PROFIT IS PRIVATIZED

"Debt"

The devil is in the details of religion.

"Devil"

Should a precious metal or stone be the common thread of civilization that determines who lives or dies?

Diamonds should not be forever.

"Diamonds"

All must die. Hopefully later rather than sooner

"Die"

Where are the rotting dinosaurs, waiting to be fracked?

"Dinosaurs"

"Diversity"

"I have dreamed all of my best dreams and life keeps making better ones that I never considered."

"Dreams"

Fentanyl is the "high of no return."

High

Some part of you, and your history, is always in the process of beginning and ending.

Process

Books and knowledge are a new battlefield in the sky of truth.

Battlefield

Truth, in the elevated minds of mankind, sends liars and lies falling to the ground in irrevelance.

Ground

Either parent drinking during a pregnancy is damaging to babies.

"Drinking"

A good education prepares you for an indefinite future.

"Education"

THE UNTIED STATES OF AMERICA

WINNING OR LOSING THE ELECTION IS NOT THE PURPOSE OF THE CAMPAIGN; DIVISIVENESS IS.

"Election"

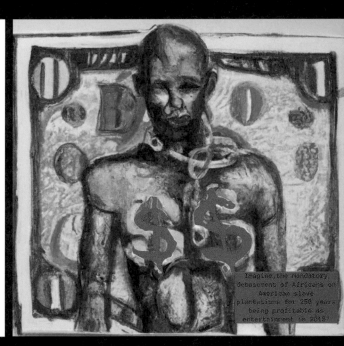

Imagine the mandatory debasement of Africans on American slave plantations for 250 years being profitable as entertainment in 2018?

"Entertainment"

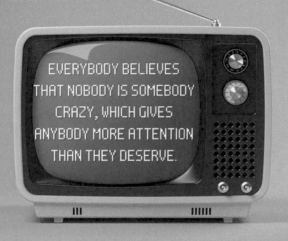

EVERYBODY BELIEVES THAT NOBODY IS SOMEBODY CRAZY, WHICH GIVES ANYBODY MORE ATTENTION THAN THEY DESERVE.

"Everybody"

FEAR

. . . is the only hope of racism

"Fear"

Stalemate wars earn no victory parades.

"Wars"

"Gerrymandering"

Gospel music is a power against evil thoughts.

"Gospel"

Broken hearts are not profitable, are they?

"Hearts"

A fatal mistake for most empires is believing intelligence is hereditary.

"Hereditary"

Being alone is an unconfirmed illusion.

"Illusion"

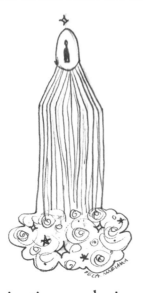

Imagination can be immortal.

"Imagination"

ALWAYS IMAGINE ALL THAT IS NOT THERE FIRST.

"Imagine"

Plantation indoctrination lasted three centuries. Mental illness still has not been considered as an affect of plantation subjectivity.

"Indoctrination"

JESUS IS A SYMBOL OF GOODWILL TOWARD ALL MEN, NOT A MEANS TO DIVIDE THE WORLD BASED ON SKIN TONES. IMAGINE, TRYING TO KILL DIVERSITY AND CALLING IT HOLY.

"Jesus"

Imagine, hours of preparation for brief moments in time, as a lifetime goal.

Imagine

AVOID DEMOCRACY LITE!

Democracy Lite

The greatest weapon of sedition is silence.

Sedition

It is possible to vote away your ability to complain.

Complain

"Killing"

"Language"

"Leftovers"

MANKIND IS JUST ONE OF THE OBJECTIVES OF THE UNIVERSE, AND YOU NEED NOT GO TO SPACE; JUST SHARE WHAT YOU HAVE BETTER.

"Mankind"

GOD IS ALL MATTER AND ALL THAT MATTERS.

"Matter"

"Media"

"Middle"

I know God is real when I try to criticize my life to myself and I sound like an idiot – because of all the miracles!

"Miracles"

A nation without free education, and free speech, invites fascism.

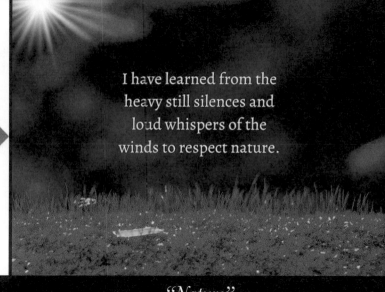

I have learned from the heavy still silences and loud whispers of the winds to respect nature.

"Nation"

"Nature"

In Defense of
NOBODY.

1. NOBODY IS AGAINST THE BIGGEST PRIVATIZED PRISON SYSTEM IN THE WORLD OR ACCIDENTAL DRONE KILLINGS.

2. NOBODY GOES TO PRISON FOR STEALING ON WALL STREET.

3. NOBODY WILL DEFINITELY TAKE ON MEDICAL POLICY DECISIONS IN RESALE OF HUMAN BODY PARTS OR EXCESSIVE MEDICAL TESTING COSTS.

4. YOU CAN COUNT ON NOBODY TO DO YOU RIGHT WHEN NOBODY IS ANSWERING.

"Nobody"

"Number 1"

"Office"

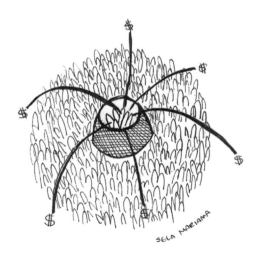

"One Percent"

"One"

A public servant embraces all the people, not just their tribe.

Servant

Imagine, a perfect union, in spite of differences.

Union

Youthful looks evaporate like a thin candy shell. It's the filling that counts.

Candy

Why should our God care about a sporting event that requires injuries, gambling, and luck?

Luck

OWNING
ANYTHING IN LIFE
FOREVER IS AN
ILLUSION OF
GRANDEUR.

"Owning"

Birth and death may be painful, so make
the best of what is between them.

"Painful"

PLAYBILL

THE NATIONAL THEATRE MAGAZINE

"THE ONE NOT TO WATCH"

EVERYBODY EVERYWHERE

5 Negative Stars

Unjust!

The Strange and Sorry Saga of a Mediocre Misanthrope

"Blackface routines without blackface makeup. A parody of failure trying to adapt to opportunity" -The HW Times

"Parody"

"Poisons"

"Polarization"

"Politics"

The right to abuse pregnant slaves cannot be discussed, but there is a name for it.

"Pregnant"

"PTSD"

"Racism"

"Reading"

"Reality"

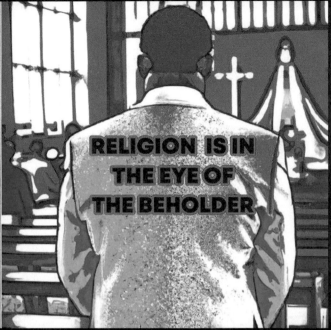

"Religion"

"Robots"

The greatest thing about art is living long enough to share it.

"Art"

"Self Pity"

Moral bankruptcy is a commodity.

Bankruptcy

Never try on handcuffs for fun.

Handcuffs

Safety is a luxury, and an illusion.

Luxury

Nobody hates your guts, but somebody does.

Hate

Religion, is sheep's clothing for wolves.

Patriotism, is sheep's clothing for gun runners.

GELA MARYAMA

I have learned from the heavy still silences and loud whispers of the winds to respect nature.

"Sheep"   *"Silences"*

Slavery is complicated by too many centuries to remember.

"Slavery"

The human spirit can shine through all time, especially in music.

"Spirit"

Sometimes storms are a death knell, and sometimes a sign of hope.

"Storms"

Stupidity, although invisible, leaves a trail . . .

"Stupidity"

Happily-ever-after is the sucker's punch of life.

"Suckers"

"THE WORST THING TO DO WHEN A MAN TREATS YOU LIKE A LADY IS ACT SURPRISED."

"Surprised"

The present and the future walked into a bar and it was tense, until the future and reality cleared the bar, with bare knuckles.

"Tense"

The Bass

It is said that it can bring about deafening applause, or inspire a wild dancing party. Sometimes it can help make tears too. Some people carry it around all their lives and suffer chronic back aches.

"The Bass"

I am a nerd of my own making.

"Nerd"

Trickle is fickle.

"Trickle"

ARE WE A RUSSIAN TROLL FARM?

"Troll"

Politics is about what is possible, not what is perfect.

Perfect

Imagine, cowboys singing the blues, because they did.

Cowboys

Respect spaceship earth, or perish in your haste and waste.

Earth

Strong melodies leave skid marks on your brain.

Melodies

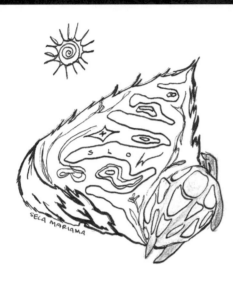

Imagine - going slower, and living longer, like a turtle.

"Turtle"

"Vibrations"

"Video Games"

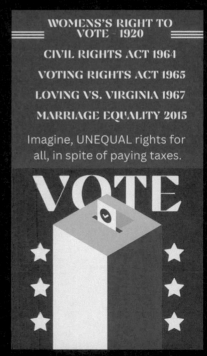

"Vote"

Poetry is the razor's edge of democracy	All the blame could be yours for me, myself, and I?
Razor	*Blame*

Wretch like me? We are not born evil, and to say so is against creation itself

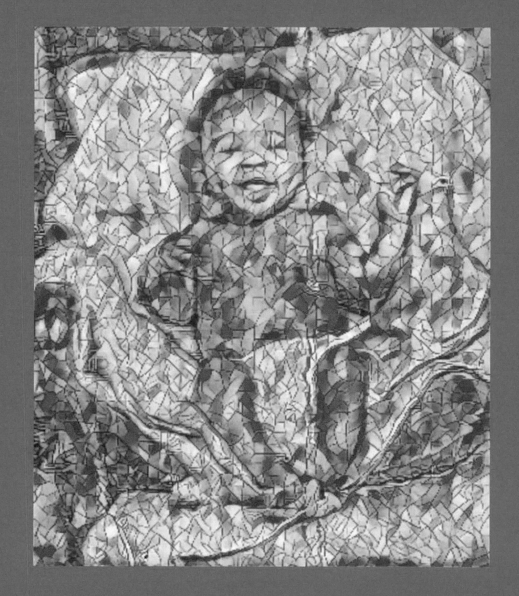

"Wretch"

About the Author

"Harley & bass in living room"

Harley White Sr., born and raised in Oakland, California, sang in local church choirs, and played classical music in the all-city high school orchestra on tuba and string bass. After high school, Harley played in jazz bands and concert marching bands while serving in the United States Air Force in the early 1960's. He holds a Bachelor of Arts in Music and a Master's of Arts degree in Music Education from Cal State University East Bay. After graduation from college, he began his teaching career, serving as a music educator for 25 years before retiring from teaching in 1999. For 10 years, Harley served as the Music program and Band Director at Alvarado Middle School in Union City, and later as a Music Director for high school choir, concert band and orchestra. He also served as a Lecturer at Holy Names College in Oakland, California, taught Jazz History at Laney Community College in Oakland, California, and taught string bass master classes at San Francisco State University.

Harley was as an elected public official and served for 6 years on the Peralta Community College District 7-member Board of Trustees. He served as Vice President of the board, and chair of the district's Facilities and Architect Committee, overseeing several facilities contracts. As a result of his time on the board Harley received several awards and commendations for his outstanding service as trustee.

Known for his vocal and jazz bass performances, Mr. White has performed with many jazz legends including Earl "Fatha" Hines, Dizzy Gillespie, Sonny Stitt, Herbie Hancock, Abby Lincoln, Max Roach, Jon Hendricks, Red Holloway, Rahsaan Roland Kirk, Dizzy Gillespie, Margie Baker, Buddy Montgomery, Tom Harrel, Ed Kelley, John Faddis, Benny Carter, Mary Stallings, Bobby Hutcherson, John Handy, Ernestine Anderson and Tony Bennett to name a few. In 1968-1969, he toured worldwide playing the bass guitar with the Edwin Hawkins Singers (the gold record hit "Oh Happy Day"), and in the mid-seventies, he toured worldwide playing the string bass with Earl "Fatha" Hines. His tuba performances included the Oakland and San Francisco Park Bands. He was a featured tuba soloist for the opening of the South San Francisco Bart Station at Colma, San Francisco - Oakland Ferry Boat Weddings and for several years with the San Francisco 49er Football Team Band, and A's Baseball Team Band. Harley also played string bass with the Oakland Symphony. In his retirement, Harley has continued to serve as a music mentor and private teacher to many musicians. He has created an internet book club with a virtual library. He is now studying piano.

1958 - High School Sousaphone

1959 - High School Graduation

1961 - Airforce Sousaphone

1961 Harley and Sousaphone

1969 Ed Hawkins Singers

1975 - Nice-France Jazz Festival

1975 - Nice Jazz Festival -2

1975 - Norway Jazz Festival - 1

1975 - Norway Jazz Festival 2

1975 Harley and Bass

1976 - Rotterdam - Fatha Hines

1976 Fatha Hines Check

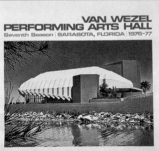

1976 Van Wezel - 1

1976 Van Wezel - 2

1977 - Graduate Degree

1976 Harley and Bass by Eddie Graham

1977 Community College
Teaching Credential

1980 Alvarado
Middle School - Fair

1980s - Mal Sharpe

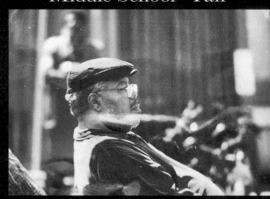

1980s - Ed Kelly

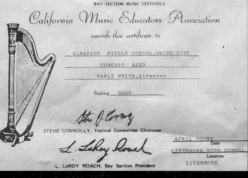

1983 Alvarado Middle
School Good

1988 - 49er Band

1986 - Alvarado Middle
School - Excellent

1989
Trustee
Award

1990s Big
Money In Jazz

1991 - Peralta AAA

1997 Jon Hendricks Bread and Roses

1999 - Learning Something Everyday

2000s - Ron Carter

LANEY COLLEGE

Instructor: Harley White

Room 189
6pm - 9pm, Mondays

History of Jazz/Blues/Pop
Course: 015A Code #0696

Course Outline: 3 Hours Lecture. Acceptance for credit CSU, UC. Historical critical analysis of the American music environment, from which its many forms have emerged and its role in social history's development of Blues, Folk, Jazz, Rock and other popular music forms in the 20th Century. 1004.00.

AA/AS Area 3; CSU CI; GETC Area 3

Preq: English Composition
Course Guide:
Required Textbook: "ALL THAT JAZZ" Author: Jack Wheaton
Publisher: Ardsley House 1994 ISBN 0-9912675-92-6

Required Video: Roots of Rythmn" Parts I,II,III 3 Hours (this video will be shown in class, as well as being available for review in the Laney Library).

Reading Assignment: Students will initially read one chapter per week for the first eight weeks of class. Students are to turn in the quiz at the end of each chapter with ALL questions stated and answered.
Lectures: Class lectures will cover materials from the chapters studied as well as videos to be shown. Notes from lectures and videos seen may be used during the final exam.

Performances: Students are expected to note material learned from possible live performances. Performers' names, songs, titles, etc. Class presentations of concertgoers will receive extra cred points.

Mid-term Exam: The mid-term will be held *April 16, 2001*, which will be short terminology quiz drawn form the first eight Chapters, of "All that Jazz", the textbook (25 Terms).

SPRING BREAK: THERE WILL BE NO CLASS ON, Monday, April 9, 2001

Mid-term Paper Due: *April 16, 2001*- An eight-page (or more) paper will be due. Please ty and use double spacing. Write your paper on the era or artist of your choice related to the Development of American Pop Music History

2002 Portrait

2001 - Laney Syallabus

2004 Big Belly Blues

Harley White Sr. DISCOGRAPHY

COVER	ALBUM	LABEL	YEAR	INSTRUMENT
	PUZZLEBOX - Jym Young's San Francisco Avantgarde	International Polydor Production	1967	Bass
	SMILEY ETC : Smiley Winters	Arhoolie Records	1969	Bass
	FILL MY CUP: The Voices of Christ of Berkeley	Savoy Records	1971	Bass
	LIVE AT BUFFALO - Earl "Fatha Hines"	Improv Records	1976	Bass

	LIVE AT BAJONES - Martha Young Allstars	Carnelian Records	1982	Bass
	ED KELLY & PHAROAH SANDERS - Ed Kelly & Pharoah Sanders	Evidence Records	1993 (Originally recorded in 1979)	Trombone
	LIVE AT RATSO'S - Earl Fatha Hines	Storyville Records	1996 (Originally recorded in 1976)	Bass
	JAZZ TOUR DE FORCE - Al Tanner	Bassinlet Music Publishing	2006	Bass

	**FIRECRACKER - Mal Sharpe's Big Money In Jazz Band with Faye Carol**	**CD Baby**	**2008**	**Bass**
	SO MANY STARS - Margie Baker	**Consolidated Artist Productions**	**2014**	**Bass**
	FILLMORE STREET LIVE - Sonny Lewis Quartet	**Sonoma Coast Records**	**2019 (Originally recorded in 1998)**	**Bass**